Degas and the Dance

THE PAINTER AND THE *PETITS RATS*, PERFECTING THEIR ART

Susan Goldman Rubin

*In association with the American Federation of Arts
and the School of American Ballet*

HARRY N. ABRAMS, INC., PUBLISHERS

Frieze of Dancers, *c. 1895. Degas painted four views of the same dancer in a wide panel called a frieze. He based his painting on drawings he made in the classroom or in his studio.*

Title page: The Rehearsal on the Stage, *c. 1874. In this pastel, Degas showed a rehearsal at the Paris Opéra. The ballet master works with the dancers while two gentleman watch from the sidelines. The scroll of the double bass at the bottom left corner suggests the orchestra.*

$\mathcal{A}$S THE YOUNG GIRLS ADJUSTED THEIR TOE SHOES
and warmed up at the barre, Edgar Degas studied them. Back at his
studio he made many drawings of the dancers in their silk tights and long
gauze skirts. "People call me the painter of dancing girls," he said.

During his long career from 1855 to 1905, Degas created more
than a thousand dance pictures. He learned that ballet training was

3

Dancers at the Barre, c. 1873. Degas often drew on colored paper. He used green when he sketched these dancers warming up.

very much like studying art. It took hard work and hours and hours of practice. Degas drew the same poses again and again, just as the dancers repeated their positions and steps again and again.

"One must repeat the same subject ten times, a hundred times," said Degas. "Nothing in art, not even movement, must seem an accident."

His group of fellow artists, the Impressionists, liked painting outdoors. With dabs of color they captured the changing effects of sunlight on people and things. Not Degas. He spent day after day *indoors*, observing at the Paris Opéra and painting in his studio.

The Dancing Class, c. 1871–72. This was one of Degas's first ballet paintings. In the center a ballerina named Josephine Gaujelin waits to do her exercises. A violinist is ready to accompany her.

Young dancers were known as *petits rats*, little rats, because of their hard life. They studied and practiced every day, hoping to become ballerinas and someday earn a living. "Most of them are poor girls doing a very demanding job," said Degas sympathetically.

In class, toe shoes tapped the wooden floor as the girls practiced *rond de jambe*. And *frappé*. And attitude. And arabesque. And again. And again. And again.

Seated Dancer, c. 1873–74.
Here Degas added touches
of white to his pencil-and-
charcoal drawing. He
observed that even when
a dancer was resting she
held her feet en pointe and
seemed to be thinking of her
steps. He ruled lines to help
him transfer the drawing
to a canvas.

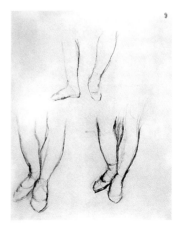

Notebook 36: Plates 8, 6,
9, 1882–85. In his note-
book Degas sometimes just
drew the dancers' feet and
legs. He wanted to under-
stand positions and move-
ments of classical ballet. A
student wrote, "Degas
showed us how to see a
dancer's foot."

A Coryphée Resting, c. 1880–82. A coryphée *was a member of the ballet company. This charcoal drawing shows a* coryphée *sitting on a bench, relaxing. Benches became an important feature in many of Degas's pictures.*

Dancer Stretching, c. 1882–85. *Degas was interested in portraying the young dancers' exhaustion as well as their movement.*

When they stopped to rest, Degas could almost feel how tired they were. He captured their gestures: stretching, yawning, rubbing their aching feet.

"Bonjour, Monsieur Degas," called the *petits rats* as they scampered to the rehearsal room. He observed the girls rushing up and down the stairs. Later, remembering what he had seen, he made many drawings.

Sometimes the dancers came to his dusty, messy studio. Degas, wearing a long smock over his suit and tie, posed them on platforms set up around the room. "Get used to drawing things from above and below," he reminded himself in his notebook.

Degas understood ballet steps so well that he would often hop

School of Ballet, c. 1873. In this oil painting Degas cut off the figures at the sides of his canvas and showed just a dancer's legs and feet coming down a spiral staircase. Figures on staircases fascinated him.

around the room mimicking an arabesque or a pirouette. "It really is very funny to see him," said a writer who visited him.

In the studio Degas enjoyed talking to the girls and listening to their gossip. "Degas found them all charming, treated them as if they were his own children, excused everything they did, and laughed at everything they said," recalled another friend.

Degas sketched and drew models in the studio, but he waited until he

9

was all alone to start a painting. He often used many of his drawings when he was composing a new painting. He would copy figures from several drawings onto one canvas to create a scene showing a group of dancers. If the work was going well, he would hum an old tune or sing an aria from one of his favorite operas.

Sometimes Degas invented his own costumes for his paintings. In

The Dancing Lesson, c. 1880. In the foreground a dancer rests on the bench, another pulls up her stocking, and a third stands holding a fan. And in the background dancers exercise at the barre. But the floor takes up as much of the painting as the dancers. "He painted admirable floors," wrote Degas's friend, the poet Paul Valéry.

the classroom, the dancers really wore plain white skirts and tops, but he added yellow and pink sashes and black throat ribbons. He needed the accents of color. Once, when Degas was giving art lessons to a friend's son, he told the young student to paint the whole canvas in tones of a

Dancer (Battement in Second Position), *1880. Degas made many drawings of the* petits rats *practicing this particular position. He kept trying to master the step just as they did—through repetition. Here he drew fifteen-year-old Melinda Darde and jotted her name on the paper.*

single color, perhaps gray or brown. "You put a little color on it, a touch here, a touch there," said Degas, "and you will see how little it takes to make it come to life."

About the time he started painting dancers, Degas had begun having trouble with his eyesight. He had gone to an eye doctor and bought a pair of

Little Girl Practicing at the Barre, *c. 1878–80. Degas wrote on this drawing, "battement in second position at the barre." He showed the dancer trying hard to achieve the correct position.*

The Ballet Class, c. 1880. A woman in a hat and lace-trimmed dress, who is probably the mother of one of the dancers, sits and reads a newspaper. Through the window behind the dancers, Degas suggests the rooftops of Paris.

The Mante Family, c. 1886. This pastel shows Madame Mante fixing her daughter Suzanne's hair before class begins. Nine-year-old Suzanne was one of the youngest petits rats to pose for Degas. Her sister Blanche, in street clothes, also entered ballet classes as a child.

blue-tinted glasses to protect his eyes from sunlight. From that point on, he was frightened that he would go blind.

But Degas forgot to worry about his eyes at the Opéra. There he kept observing and drawing the lessons and rehearsals. He sketched the *petits rats* as they practiced their steps. Occasionally he showed the mothers and big sisters waiting on the sidelines, maybe reading a newspaper.

Among the *petits rats* he drew were two sisters, Suzanne and Blanche Mante. Many years later, Suzanne remembered him fondly as a "quiet,

13

The Dance Class, *1874. A year after beginning his first version of* The Dance Class, *Degas did another based on his many drawings. This one also includes the famous dancer and choreographer Jules Perrot. Here one of the dancers performs an arabesque under his watchful eye. A music stand is in the foreground.*

The Ballet Master, Jules Perrot, *1875. Degas made this study for* The Dance Class *with a medium called essence, which is oil paint thinned with turpentine. He repeated the drawing in his painting.*

The Dance Class, *c. 1873–76. Mothers and chaperones sit in the far end of the room. Jules Perrot directs the* corps de ballet *while a little dog sees his reflection in a watering can. Degas used many of his drawings to compose this painting, including one of the ballet master.*

kind old man who wore blue spectacles." Others thought Degas was cranky, interested only in art.

Degas admired the choreographer Jules Perrot and portrayed him in two versions of *The Dance Class.* In one, he included a watering can, used in those days to sprinkle water on the wood floor so that the ballerinas would not slip.

Dancer in Walking Position with Arms Stretched Forward, *c. 1878–80. Degas sketched this unknown dancer in charcoal.*

Dancers Practicing at the Barre, *1877. Once again the floor took up most of the painting. One critic considered this "perhaps the finest of all" Degas's dance paintings.*

Degas featured a watering can in another painting, *Dancers Practicing at the Barre.* He gave this one to his friend Henri Rouart. Degas had given Rouart a different picture, a pastel, but took it back to make it better. However, Degas reworked the picture so much that he wound up spoiling it. In exchange, he gave Rouart *Dancers Practicing at the Barre.* Yet Degas was not satisfied with that one, either. "Decidedly that watering can is idiotic," he said. "I really must get rid of it."

But the story goes that Rouart, determined to hold on to his gift, chained the painting to the wall so that Degas could not remove it!

16

Ballet Studio at the Opéra in Rue Le Peletier, *1872. In this oil painting a dancer performs for her teacher, Louis Merante. Degas showed the class taking place in the old Paris Opéra. Although the building burned down a year later, Degas continued to picture its archways, mirrors, and long doors.*

"He felt a work could never be called finished," remembered Degas's friend, the poet Paul Valéry. Degas was a perfectionist.

Degas preferred giving his pictures to friends rather than selling them. Nevertheless, when he needed money he sold some of his work through his dealers. By the time Degas was fifty, many important collectors competed to buy his ballet paintings and drawings. "When

Rehearsal in the Studio, *1874. Dancers follow the ballet master; in those days a violinist accompanied them. Tall windows of the Paris Opéra appear in this painting, along with a big section of floor. Degas used spaces of floor to draw the viewer into the picture.*

your eyes are trained on those leaping figures, they all come to life," wrote a critic. "You can almost hear the dancing mistress: 'Heels forward . . . hold up your wrists.'"

In the late 1870s, Degas worked more and more with pastels rather than painting in oils. He loved using the colored chalks because he could combine areas of color with line. With his fingers he blended vivid tones of blue-green, peach, and orange in the skirt of the *Swaying Dancer.* Then, with a delicate line, he picked out details: the ruffles of the dancer's

Swaying Dancer (Dancer in Green), *1877–79. Degas composed this picture at an unusual angle, on a diagonal, as though he were looking at the dancers from above. He featured one ballerina in the center and showed only the legs and tutus of the others.*

Dancer on Point: The Star, c. 1878. The ballerina stands en pointe with her arms extended. With pastels Degas captured the flurry of her movement as she steps into an arabesque.

tutu, the shape of her leg, an outline of her toe shoe. He described pastel as "the powder of a butterfly's wings." He experimented by mixing pastels with charcoal and tempera paint, or bleaching his drawings in sunlight to lighten and soften the colors. Sometimes he blew steam over the paper to make the drawing look smeared.

When Degas was not working in his studio, he went to the Opéra to observe. He still wanted to show the *petits rats* training to become ballerinas. He admired their dedication. Degas wrote a poem called "Little Dancer" that began:

> Dance, winged scamp, dance on the wooden lawns,
> Love only that—let dancing be your life.

Once or twice a year, at age ten or eleven, the girls took an exam. This was the most terrifying day of the whole year, recalled Suzanne Mante. The girls had to perform all alone on an empty stage, accompanied by a pianist. Their teachers, mothers, and the ballet master sat in the front rows of the Opéra, watching. Only the girls who did well were promoted.

Even after years of painting the *petits rats*, Degas had never attended an exam. When he finally did, he took notes. "It is the age when dancing is pretty," he scribbled. "The

Dancer Executing Tendu à la Seconde, *c. 1885. Degas drew a study in brown chalk of this dancer practicing her step.*

21

Dance Examination, *1880. Degas's housekeeper posed as the "stage mother" for this pastel. The contrast between the dancers and the outside world of mothers and audience greatly interested Degas.*

Waiting, c. 1882. This pastel also reflects the difference between the two worlds of the dancer and her "stage mother" or chaperone. Here the figures sit side by side on a bench, but each is lost in her own separate thoughts. Hunched over, they seem ready to spring up as soon as they are called.

jury claps frequently." In two of his drawings Degas portrayed the moments just before the test. *Dance Examination* pictures a mother fluffing out her daughter's skirt as the girl pulls up her stocking. In *Waiting,* a dancer who has not had her turn yet sits slumped on a

23

Dancers in Repose, c. 1898. This
pastel shows dancers taking a
break before they perform.

bench beside her mother or chaperone, who stares dully at an umbrella.

Degas noticed everything—he understood the ballerinas' jitters as they got ready to go onstage. But he also captured the thrill of a successful performance.

During the late 1880s Degas realized that his eyes were getting weaker. To save his eyes for artwork, he wrote letters with his eyes half closed and examined drawings with a magnifying glass.

Yellow Dancers (In the Wings), *1874–76. Degas often portrayed the moments just before a performance, as in this oil painting. When he worked in oils, he experimented by applying and blending paint with his fingers, as well as his brushes.*

For his drawings, he used black crayon and charcoal instead of pencil because the marks they made were easier on his eyes. He found it harder to see outlines, so his pastels from this time look fuzzy and abstract. Despite his difficulties, he was eager to work. "I still dream of projects," he wrote.

On days when Degas could not see well enough to draw or paint, he modeled figures in wax as he had done early in his career. Once,

Dancers, c. 1903. Toward the end of his career when his eyesight was failing, Degas's pastels looked more blurred. Color and movement became more important than details such as the faces of the dancers.

The Dancer on Stage, c. 1876–77. Degas created this picture by drawing with pastels over a print he had made. The star, or prima ballerina, leaps toward the orchestra pit so vigorously that one critic said that if he had been the conductor of the orchestra, he would have been ready to catch her if she fell.

Russian Dancers, c. 1899. Degas made pastels of Russian dancers in groups of three. The dancers wear brightly colored skirts and garlands of flowers in their hair. The pictures were probably inspired by operas that included Russian folk dances.

opposite, Orchestra Musicians, 1870–71. In this oil painting Degas features the musicians of the orchestra in the foreground. But through light, color, and composition, he focuses attention on the smiling ballerina as she takes her bows after a triumphant performance.

when his model Pauline was posing for him, she got tired of standing on one foot and needed a rest. While she stood near the stove warming herself, she asked Degas to teach her the tune he had just been singing.

"Of course, my girl," he said. "I'll sing it for you." As Degas sang, he made little bows and danced a few steps. And Pauline, laughing, returned the bow. "Degas seemed quite happy," she remembered.

He did his last dance drawings, *Russian Dancers*, from 1899 to 1905, when he was in his late sixties. The drawings show the dancers gaily kicking up the heels of their red boots.

In his art Degas captured the joy of dance for all time. The *petits rats* live on in his drawings and paintings forever, and even today dancers recognize themselves in his work. "Drawing," Degas once said, "is not what one sees, but what one can make others see."

Edgar Degas
A Brief Biography

Self-Portrait, c. 1857–58. Degas was in his early twenties when he painted this picture. He not only captured a likeness; he seems to show the kind of person he was—gentle and observant.

HILAIRE-GERMAINE EDGAR DEGAS, one of the greatest artists of the nineteenth century, was born on July 19, 1834, in Paris, France. Edgar was the oldest of five children, three brothers and two sisters. When he was just thirteen his mother died, and his father, Auguste, never remarried.

Edgar adored his young, fun-loving mother and missed her dreadfully, but he soon became used to living in a family dominated by bachelors. Auguste, a distant yet caring father, earned his living as a banker. However, he loved art and took Edgar with him to see great paintings at the Musée du Louvre.

At age twelve Edgar went to boarding school in Paris and, like many of his classmates, took extra lessons in drawing once a week. When he was nineteen he entered law school, to please his father. But Edgar did not want to be a lawyer. "I want to be a painter!" he announced. His father was horrified—being an artist was no way to earn a living. Edgar moved into a miserable attic to prove that he meant what he said. His father relented and gave his approval of his son's new career.

Edgar Degas began his training by copying works of the great masters that hung in the Louvre and in the Musée de Luxembourg, the world's first museum of contemporary art. His idol was the artist Jean-Auguste-Dominique Ingres. Once Degas met Ingres, who told him, "Draw lines, young man, lots of lines, either from memory or from nature." Degas took this advice and became an outstanding draftsman.

At age twenty-one Degas briefly attended Ecole des Beaux-Arts (School of Fine Arts), but he dropped out and studied privately with professors of art. During this period he made many drawings and paintings of his sisters and brothers, as well as self-portraits. In the summer of 1856 he went to Naples, Italy, his father's birthplace, and stayed at his grandfather's huge villa. While there Degas sketched and painted pictures of his relatives. His studies of his favorite aunt, Laura, and her husband and daughters later evolved into one of his masterpieces, *The Bellelli Family*. After three years in Italy, Degas returned to Paris and began a series of paintings depicting historical scenes. Then, in 1865, he turned once again to doing portraits. Around this time he became interested in painting scenes of contemporary life around him—theater, concerts, and horse races. At the racetrack he sketched the spectators, as well as the jockeys on horseback. In his studio Degas modeled small sculptures of horses to help him understand the figures in three dimensions.

In 1867, when he was thirty-three years old, he made his first ballet painting, *The Source*. It was based on a real

30

ballet, a fairy tale that featured a live horse on the stage. Degas put the horse in his painting. During the next few years he did more ballet paintings of performances, and by the early 1870s, Degas had started to go behind the scenes at the Paris Opéra.

Degas had been working hard at his art for many years, and he needed a rest. In 1872, he traveled to the United States for a visit to New Orleans, Louisiana, where his mother had been born. His brother René lived there, working in the family's cotton business. At first, Degas loved New Orleans. "Everything attracts me here," he wrote. He started a large picture of the family's office, *The Cotton Market in New Orleans*, that included portraits of his grandfather and two brothers. But he finished the painting in Paris, for after a few months of traveling, Degas felt homesick. He especially missed the opera and ballet, and wanted to be back in time for a performance by one of his favorite dancers.

The artists' community in Paris was brimming with new ideas. Degas and other modern French artists had recently seen prints from Japan—full of unusual viewpoints and strange angles—for the first time. The prints inspired Degas with fresh ideas for composition. Photographs influenced him, too. Degas had become excited about the new process of photography, first introduced around 1848, and he experimented with his own camera.

He also sometimes sculpted figures in clay and wax. One of his best-known works was a small statue, *Little Dancer of Fourteen Years*. The model, Marie Van Goethen, was a *petit rat* at the Paris Opéra ballet school. Degas painted the wax figurine, dressed it in a tutu, and added real hair braided and tied with a ribbon. When he exhibited the sculpture in 1874, it created a sensation. The wax figure looked so lifelike it startled people and disturbed them. "Why is she so ugly?" asked a dismayed critic. But Degas wanted to show dancers as they really were.

Degas often used ordinary women as his models. From dancers and singers, to laundresses and shop girls, Degas portrayed women at work. His circle of friends included female artists such as Berthe Morisot and Mary Cassatt. Yet he never married and had no children. "I was in love with art," he said later, looking back on his life.

Degas lived alone. He fussed constantly about his health, and though he enjoyed delicious food, he told his housekeeper to cook plain meals because he believed that diet was good for him. Even his close friends thought he was a worrywart. They knew he had odd habits. When invited to a dinner party, Degas gave his host strict instructions: No flowers on the table. No cats or dogs in the dining room. No perfume on the women. "And very few lights," he said.

As a young man Degas began having trouble with his eyes, and his condition kept growing worse. At the end of his life he was almost blind. He would run his hand along his paintings to feel the smooth texture. He would praise a picture by saying, "It is flat like all beautiful painting."

In 1912, when he was seventy-eight, Degas stopped working altogether and spent his time strolling alone through the streets of his beloved Paris. "My legs are good. I walk well," he said. But Degas used a cane. And his eyesight was probably just clear enough to let him see curbs and cross streets by himself.

In the last year of his life Degas became ill and had to stay in bed. When he died in 1917, his tombstone read, "He loved drawing very much."

Dancer Executing Port de Bras, *c. 1880. In black chalk and pastel Degas captured a dancer taking a bow.*

Author's Note

I love ballet, and I love the art of Edgar Degas. So I was delighted to write a book for young people about Degas's paintings of dancers. Growing up in New York I went to ballet performances on special occasions. Like many girls my age, I dreamed of someday becoming a ballerina. However, I didn't qualify—I had flat feet. So I settled for studying modern dance, then art, and attending performances of American Ballet Theater and the New York City Ballet Company. But finally, in researching this book, a dream came true: I went behind the scenes and visited the classes at the School of American Ballet at Lincoln Center.

Like Degas, I sat on the sidelines and observed talented young dancers practicing *plié, rond de jambe,* and *pique*. The director of the school sat with me and in whispers explained what the girls were doing. I jotted down the names of the steps and comments from the teachers. It was like seeing Degas's drawings and paintings come to life. Later, when I began writing this book, I remembered what I had seen and imagined myself in Degas's place as he studied the *petits rats* at the Paris Opéra.

I hope that readers who are dancers will recognize themselves in Degas's art. And for those of us who must enjoy ballet from the audience, I present this book as a celebration of dance and the brilliant, eternally glowing art of Edgar Degas.

—Susan Goldman Rubin

Special thanks to Jeanne Lunin, Kay Mazzo, Suki Schorer, Antonina Tumskovsky, Amy Bordy, and Thomas W. Schoff of the School of American Ballet, and to Michaelyn Mitchell and Anne Palermo of the American Federation of Arts.

To my favorite ballerinas: Maddie, Naomi, Elizabeth, Rebecca, and Amy

Bibliography

*Armstrong, Carol. *A Degas Sketchbook*. With a postscript by David Hockney. Los Angeles: The J. Paul Getty Trust, 2000.

Boggs, Jean Sutherland. *Degas*. New York: Metropolitan Museum of Art, and Ottawa: National Gallery of Canada, 1988.

Browse, Lillian. *Degas Dancers*. Boston Book and Art Shop. New York: Studio Publications, c. 1948.

*Degas, Edgar. *Degas by Himself: Drawings, Prints, Paintings, Writings*. Boston: Little, Brown and Co., 1987.

Degas: The Man and His Art. Discoveries series. New York: Harry N. Abrams, 1993.

Gordon, Robert, and Andrew Forge. *Degas*. New York: Harry N. Abrams, 1988.

*Halévy, Daniel. *My Friend Degas*. Middletown: Wesleyan University Press, 1964.

McMullen, Roy. *Degas: His Life, Times, and Work*. Boston: Houghton Mifflin Co., 1984.

*Meyer, Susan. *Edgar Degas*. First Impressions series. New York: Harry N. Abrams, 1994.

*Valéry, Paul. *Degas Dance Drawing*. New York: Prestel, 1997.

Schacherl, Lillian. *Edgar Degas: Dancers and Nudes*. Munich and New York: Prestel, 1997.

Books about ballet:

Gresovic, Robert. *Ballet 101*. New York: Hyperion, 1998.

*Kirstein, Lincoln. *The Classic Ballet: Basic Technique and Terminology*. New York: Alfred A. Knopf, 1952, and Gainesville: University Press of Florida, 1998.

———. *Dance: A Short History of Classic Theatrical Dancing*. Princeton: A Dance Horizons Book, 1987.

———. *Four Centuries of Ballet: Fifty Masterworks*. New York: Dover Publications, Inc., 1984.

* indicates books suitable for young readers

The text is set in 16-point Bodoni Classic.

Library of Congress Cataloging-in-Publication Data

Rubin, Susan Goldman. Degas and the dance / Rubin, Susan Goldman. p. cm. Includes bibliographical references. Summary: Explores the life and work of the nineteenth-century French artist who devoted most of his artwork to the subject of ballet. ISBN 0-8109-0567-1 I. Degas, Edgar, 1834–1917—Juvenile literature. 2. Painters—France—Biography—Juvenile literature. 3. Dancers in art—Juvenile literature. [1. Degas, Edgar, 1834-1917. 2. Artists. 3. Painting, French. 4. Dancers in art.] I. Title: Edgar Degas. II. Title. ND553.D3 R83 2002 7594—dc21 2001006580

Text copyright © 2002 Susan Goldman Rubin Illustrations copyright © 2002 American Federation of Arts. For individual art credits, please see below.

Published in 2002 by Harry N. Abrams, Incorporated, New York

All rights reserved. No part of the contents of this book maybe reproduced without the written permission of the publisher.

Printed and bound in Hong Kong

10 9 8 7 6 5 4 3 2

American Federation of Arts, 41 E. 65th Street, New York, NY 10021

Harry N. Abrams, Inc., 100 Fifth Avenue, New York, N.Y. 10011, www.abramsbooks.com Abrams is a division of LA MARTINIÈRE GROUPE